LET YOUR HEARTS BE BROKEN

THE PASSIO SERIES

Let your hearts be broken
A JOURNEY THROUGH THE SUNDAYS OF LENT YEAR A IN PREPARATION FOR EASTER

Gerard O'Brien CP

First published in 2004 by
the columba press
55A Spruce Avenue, Stillorgan Industrial Park,
Blackrock, Co Dublin

Cover by Bill Bolger
Origination by The Columba Press
Printed in Ireland by ColourBooks Ltd, Dublin

ISBN 1 85607 470 6

Acknowledgements

Scripture texts are taken from *The Jerusalem Bible*, copyright © 1966, 1967, 1968 by Darton, Longman and Todd Ltd and Doubleday and Co Inc, and used by permission. Quotations from *The Roman Missal* are copyright © 1969, 1970, 1973 by The International Committee on English in the Liturgy Inc. All rights reserved. Used by permission.

Copyright © 2004, Gerard O'Brien CP

Table of Contents

Introduction	7
Ash Wednesday	9
Group Meeting before the First Sunday of Lent	12
Readings for First Sunday of Lent	14
First Week of Lent	17
Group Meeting before the Second Sunday	22
Readings for the Second Sunday of Lent	24
Second Week of Lent	26
Group Meeting before the Third Sunday	31
Readings for the Third Sunday of Lent	33
Third Week of Lent	36
Group Meeting before the Fourth Sunday	41
Readings for the Fourth Sunday of Lent	43
Fourth Week of Lent	46
Group Meeting before the Fifth Sunday	51
Readings for the Fifth Sunday of Lent	53
Fifth Week of Lent	56
Group Meeting before Passion Sunday	61
Readings for Passion Sunday	63
Holy Week	67
Holy Thursday	70
Good Friday	71
Holy Saturday – The Easter Vigil	72
Group Meeting	73

Introduction

Lent is the season the church dedicates to delving more deeply into the mystery of the love of God celebrated in the passion, death and resurrection of Jesus. It is a time to allow the Spirit of the risen Lord to break our hearts once more with the power of love, renewing and converting us to the ways of the living God.

The Passio Series works through celebrating the presence of the Lord on a daily basis by attending to a given spiritual exercise which awakens and helps us remember that the risen Jesus walks with us during this time. It is he who renews and converts us.

Each day, from Monday to Friday, an exercise of prayer and reflection is offered in light of a chosen weekly theme, along with a 'Personal Exercise' to help focus this activity. Each daily exercise leads to a 'Lenten Prayer' and a line of sacred scripture given at the foot of each page. These short scriptural quotations have been chosen because they capture the theme of the week and can easily be committed to memory.

The idea is to remember the quote of scripture for each day as often as is practically possible. In this way the theme and the presence of Jesus will be recalled because it is his voice that is heard when the sacred scriptures are attended to in faith. Saturday is seen as a day to take stock and reflect on the past week.

Since the daily exercises have also been shaped as a preparation for the coming Sunday celebration of the eucharist, the Passio approach ensures that Sunday Mass is experienced as the source and summit of the life of faith.

Passio thus helps to awaken and remember the presence of the risen Lord seven days a week. It also respects the Sunday eucharist as the centre of the life of faith celebrated as the Feast of the Resurrection.

The themes chosen for our Lenten journey are: Jesus helps us to overcome sin and temptation; Jesus casts out all fear; Jesus is the Water of Life; Jesus gives us eyes of faith; Life in the Spirit of Jesus; and Jesus reveals God's love for us.

For each of the weeks of Lent a group faith sharing session, based on the weekly theme, is given along with the relevant Sunday readings. The structure of the meeting is also designed to reflect the coming celebration of the Sunday eucharist – whilst at the same time allowing each person who participates the opportunity to discover the presence of the Lord in their own life story.

To this end, individuals are invited to share how the risen Lord is working in their life. This sharing is to be revered and respected. Any dialogue to help tease out a person's search for meaning is to be conducted in mutual love. We must ever remember that love is the hallmark of all we say and do in the name of the Lord.

Passio helps us to awaken and nurture the presence of Jesus as the heart of the faith that binds us together in his church. Our Christian living consists in following him as our Way, our Truth, and our Life. In short, the heart of our faith is the person of Jesus.

May the God of Jesus Christ pour the Holy Spirit into your minds and hearts during this season of Lent so that the love of God shown in the passion, death and resurrection of Jesus will overwhelm you, transforming both you, and your loved ones, into a perfect communion of love rooted in the mystery of the Most Holy Trinity.

ASH WEDNESDAY

Jesus helps us to overcome sin and temptation

A reading from the letter of St Paul to the Romans
Sin entered the world through one man, and through sin death, and thus death has spread through the whole human race because everyone has sinned. If it is certain that death reigned over everyone as the consequence of one man's fall, it is even more certain that one man, Jesus Christ, will cause everyone to reign in life who receives the free gift that he does not deserve, of being made righteous. Again, as one man's fall brought condemnation on everyone, so the good act of one man brings everyone life and makes them justified. As by one man's disobedience many were made sinners, so by one man's obedience many will be made righteous.

Living in Christ
We are put in right relationship with God the Father through living out our relationship with the risen Lord in response to the Holy Spirit. This is what it means to say 'Jesus Christ will cause everyone to reign in life'. Through our baptism we share in the victory which Christ has won – overcoming sin and death. Our personal, living relationship with Jesus is the free gift that brings us true and everlasting life.

Personal Exercise
Spend some time reflecting on the truth that it is only by awakening and remembering our relationship with Jesus that we can grow in authentic love and overcome sin and temptation.

Lenten Prayer
Let us pray for the grace to fight sin and selfishness in our lives by always remembering God's love for us in Christ Jesus.
We ask this through Christ our Lord Amen.

Jesus has offered one single sacrifice for sins. *Hebrews 10:12*

Jesus helps us to overcome sin and temptation

A reading from the holy Gospel according to Matthew
Jesus was led by the Spirit out into the wilderness to be tempted by the devil. He fasted for forty days and forty nights, after which he was very hungry, and the tempter came and said to him, 'If you are the Son of God, tell these stones to turn into loaves.' But he replied, 'Scripture says: Man does not live on bread alone but on every word that comes from the mouth of God.'

The devil then took him to the holy city and made him stand on the parapet of the Temple. 'If you are the Son of God,' he said 'throw yourself down; for scripture says: He will put you in his angels' charge, and they will support you on their hands in case you hurt your foot against a stone.' Jesus said to him, 'Scripture also says: You must not put the Lord your God to the test.'

Jesus is tempted by the devil
When it comes to temptation scripture tells us that even Jesus was tried. What Jesus shows us is that in times of temptation we can overcome it by remembering the presence of the living God. The good news for us is that the risen Lord is always with us. In times of temptation we are to awaken Jesus' Holy Spirit of love within us and thus overcome sin and temptation through our bond with him.

Personal Exercise
Awaken in yourself the awareness of continually living in good faith through your willingness to be led by the Holy Spirit of love.

Lenten Prayer
Let us pray to choose to always act in good faith through awakening our faith in God's only Son.
We ask this through Christ our Lord. Amen.

Happy the person who stands firm when trials come. *James 1:12*

FRIDAY AFTER ASH WEDNESDAY

Jesus helps us to overcome sin and temptation

A reading from the holy Gospel according to Matthew
Next, taking Jesus to a very high mountain, the devil showed him all the kingdoms of the world and their splendour. 'I will give you all these,' he said, 'if you fall at my feet and worship me.' Then Jesus replied, 'Be off, Satan! For scripture says: You must worship the Lord your God, and serve him alone.' Then the devil left him, and angels appeared and looked after him.

Jesus calls us to worship and serve the Lord
In response to the devil's temptation of offering him the trappings of power and prestige in this world, Jesus reminds the devil that all creatures are to give God his rightful place and worship and serve the Lord God. As Christians we are called to choose the way of self-sacrificing love – revealed to us most fully in the death and resurrection of Jesus – as opposed to the way of self-indulgence and egotistical power. It is our belief that true happiness can only be found by giving God in Christ Jesus his rightful place in our lives. This is especially true for us as members of the church who form a community of sincere worship and loving service.

Personal exercise
Choose to make several acts of prayer and self-sacrificing love throughout your day.

Lenten Prayer
Let us pray for the grace to reflect the prayerfulness and self-sacrificing love of Jesus in our lives.
We ask this through Christ our Lord. Amen.

You must worship the Lord your God and serve him alone.
Matthew 4:10

GROUP MEETING BEFORE FIRST SUNDAY OF LENT

Gathering as the tiny church.
Some moments of relaxation and becoming quiet.
Proclamation of the Word of God: Readings for the First Sunday of Lent.

Questions for sharing in dialogue
The purpose of Lent is to understand more deeply the meaning of Jesus' death and resurrection and to learn from the living God how to reflect the depth of this love in our lives. How do you feel as you enter into the discipline of Lent once more? How has your understanding of what Lent is about grown or changed? How can you travel the path of Lent so as to grow in understanding of your living relationship with the risen Lord?
Relaxing music to be played as questions are reflected upon to allow you to find meaning through, with, and in the Word of God.

From dialogue to praise
Once stories and any relevant dialogue have been shared the person leading the session says: As we begin our journey of Lent we remember the risen Lord is with us. He will lead us to a greater understanding of the meaning of his death and resurrection. He will teach us how to love.

Liturgical Memory
We remember it is Jesus himself who teaches us how to overcome sin and temptation and so purify our minds and hearts in God's love. We recall the words the priest prays on our behalf as we begin our Lenten journey:
    Father, all-powerful and ever-living God,
    we do well always and everywhere to give you thanks
    through Jesus Christ our Lord.
    His fast of forty days makes this a holy season of self-denial.
    By rejecting the devil's temptations he has taught us
    to rid ourselves of the hidden corruption of evil,
    and so to share his paschal meal in purity of heart,
    until we come to its fulfilment in the promised land of heaven.

Now we join the angels and the saints as they sing
their unending hymn of praise: Holy, holy, holy...

Living Word
We remember Jesus reveals the love of God to us and shows us how to grow in that love. We listen to his voice as he instructs us in love, saying: You must worship the Lord your God.

(Name), Jesus speaks these words to you:
You must worship the Lord your God.

Quiet time/Intercessions

Closing Prayer
Let us pray with confidence to the Father in the words our Saviour gave us: Our Father ...

Blessing
Lord, bless your people and make them holy
so that, avoiding evil, they may find you
the fulfilment of their longing.
We ask this through Christ our Lord. Amen.

The Lord grant us a quiet night and a perfect end. Amen.

A reading from the book of Genesis
The creation, temptation and sin of our first parents.

The Lord God fashioned man of dust from the soil. Then he breathed into his nostrils a breath of life, and thus man became a living being. The Lord God planted a garden in Eden which is in the east, and there he put the man he had fashioned. The Lord God caused to spring up from the soil every kind of tree, enticing to look at and good to eat, with the tree of life and the tree of the knowledge of good and evil in the middle of the garden.

The serpent was the most subtle of all the wild beasts that the Lord God had made. It asked the woman, 'Did God really say you were not to eat from any of the trees in the garden?' The woman answered the serpent, 'We may eat the fruit of the trees in the garden. But of the fruit of the tree in the middle of the garden God said, "You must not eat it, nor touch it, under pain of death".' Then the serpent said to the woman, 'No! You will not die! God knows in fact that on the day you eat it your eyes will be opened and you will be like gods, knowing good and evil.' The woman saw that the tree was good to eat and pleasing to the eye, and that it was desirable for the knowledge that it could give. So she took some of its fruit and ate it. She gave some also to her husband who was with her, and he ate it. Then the eyes of both of them were opened and they realised that they were naked. So they sewed fig-leaves together to make themselves loin-cloths.
This is the word of the Lord.

Responsorial Psalm
Response: Have mercy on us, O Lord, for we have sinned.

> Have mercy on me, God, in your kindness.
> In your compassion blot out my offence.
> O wash me more and more from my guilt
> and cleanse me from my sin. R.

> My offences truly I know them;
> my sin is always before me.
> Against you, you alone, have I sinned;
> what is evil in your sight I have done. R.
>
> A pure heart create for me, O God,
> put a steadfast spirit within me.
> Do not cast me away from your presence,
> nor deprive me of your holy spirit. R.
>
> Give me again the joy of your help;
> with a spirit of fervour sustain me.
> O Lord, open my lips
> and my mouth shall declare your praise. R.

A reading from the first letter of St Paul to the Romans
The risen Jesus brings everyone life.

Sin entered the world through one man, and through sin death, and thus death has spread through the whole human race because everyone has sinned. If it is certain that death reigned over everyone as the consequence of one man's fall, it is even more certain that one man, Jesus Christ, will cause everyone to reign in life who receives the free gift that he does not deserve, of being made righteous. Again, as one man's fall brought condemnation on everyone, so the good act of one man brings everyone life and makes them justified. As by one man's disobedience many were made sinners, so by one man's obedience many will be made righteous.
This is the word of the Lord.

> Praise to you, O Christ, king of eternal glory!
> Man does not live on bread alone,
> but on every word that comes from the mouth of God.
> Praise to you, O Christ, king of eternal glory!

A reading from the holy Gospel according to Matthew
Jesus was led to the wilderness by the Spirit and was tempted.

Jesus was led by the Spirit out into the wilderness to be tempted by the devil. He fasted for forty days and forty nights, after which he was very hungry, and the tempter came and said to him, 'If you are the Son of God, tell these stones to turn into loaves.' But he replied, 'Scripture says:
Man does not live on bread alone
but on every word that comes from the mouth of God.'

The devil then took him to the holy city and made him stand on the parapet of the Temple. 'If you are the Son of God' he said, 'throw yourself down; for scripture says:
He will put you in his angels' charge,
and they will support you on their hands
in case you hurt your foot against a stone.'

Jesus said to him, 'Scripture also says: You must not put the Lord your God to the test.'
Next, taking him to a very high mountain, the devil showed him all the kingdoms of the world and their splendour. 'I will give you all these,' he said, 'if you fall at my feet and worship me.' Then Jesus replied, 'Be off, Satan! For scripture says: You must worship the Lord your God, and serve him alone.'
Then the devil left him, and angels appeared and looked after him.
This is the Gospel of the Lord.

Jesus casts out all fear

A reading from the book of Genesis
The Lord said to Abram, 'Leave your country, your family and your father's house, for the land I will show you. I will make you a great nation; I will bless you and make your name so famous that it will be used as a blessing. I will bless those who bless you: I will curse those who slight you. All the tribes of the earth shall bless themselves by you.' So Abram went as the Lord told him.

The call of the living God
Abram is called by the Lord and responds in total faith to God's call in his life. Today, we too are called by the living God. We listen to God in Christ calling us when we are attentive to the risen Lord revealed to us through the proclamation of sacred scripture and the celebration of the gift of the sacraments. Our faith is the response we make to this call. When we awaken our faith in Jesus this dispels all fear because through Jesus we know the God of love is with us. The love of God in Christ casts out all fear from our lives.

Personal Exercise
Reflect on the truth that your Christian faith is the response you make to the revelation of God's love revealed through the Word of God, Jesus Christ.

Lenten Prayer
Let us pray for the grace to awaken the gift of faith given to us through the sacrament of baptism.
We ask this through Christ our Lord. Amen.

It is impossible to please God without faith. *Hebrews 11:6*

Jesus casts out all fear

A reading from the book of Psalms

> The word of the Lord is faithful
> and all his works to be trusted.
> The Lord loves justice and right
> and fills the earth with his love.
>
> The Lord looks on those who revere him,
> on those who hope in his love,
> to rescue their souls from death,
> to keep them alive in famine.
>
> Our soul is waiting for the Lord.
> The Lord is our help and our shield.
> May your love be upon us, O Lord,
> as we place all our hope in you.

The God of love is our hope
God's presence lives in our lives as both a help and our shield. In other words Jesus is always with us to help us and protect us.

Personal Exercise
When you read sacred scripture today, cultivate the sense of prayerfulness within you to allow a dialogue between yourself and the risen Lord to occur.

Lenten Prayer
Let us pray to put time aside each day to listen to God's living Word, Jesus Christ.
We ask this through Christ our Lord. Amen.

Your faith has saved you. *Luke 7:50*

FIRST WEEK OF LENT: WEDNESDAY

Jesus casts out all fear

A reading from the second letter of St Paul to Timothy
With me, bear the hardships for the sake of the good news, relying on the power of God who has saved us and called us to be holy – not because of anything we ourselves have done but for his own purposes and by his own grace. This grace had already been granted to us, in Christ Jesus, before the beginning of time, but it has only been revealed by the appearing of our saviour Christ Jesus. He abolished death, and he has proclaimed life and immortality through the good news.

Christ Jesus is the Good News
St Paul urges us to rely totally on the power of God's love that has been freely given in Christ Jesus. It is the person of the risen Christ who is the good news. It is this mystery of his risen person that is made present in the proclamation of sacred scripture and the celebration of the sacraments of the church. Jesus is the heart and centre of our faith. Jesus casts out all fear from our lives. Only he can lead us to the love of the Father in the Spirit and cause us to share in the life of the Holy Trinity.

Personal Exercise
Re-appraise the degree to which you are attentive to the risen Lord in your life through the priority you give to the act of personal prayer.

Lenten Prayer
Let us pray for the grace to be more attentive to the revelation of love given to us through the Word of God, Jesus Christ.
We ask this through Christ our Lord. Amen.

I live in faith: faith in the Son of God. *Galatians 2:20*

Jesus casts out all fear

A reading from the holy Gospel according to Matthew
Jesus took with him Peter and James and his brother John and led them up a high mountain where they could be alone. There in their presence he was transfigured; his face shone like the sun and his clothes became as white as the light.

Suddenly Moses and Elijah appeared to them; they were talking with him. Then Peter spoke to Jesus. 'Lord,' he said, 'it is wonderful for us to be here; if you wish, I will make three tents here, one for you, one for Moses and one for Elijah.'

He was still speaking when suddenly a bright cloud covered them with shadow, and from the cloud there came a voice which said, 'This is my Son, the Beloved; he enjoys my favour. Listen to him.'

God the Father speaks
The Father's voice tells us that Jesus is his Son and that we are to listen to him. The good news is that simple. Jesus is the Son of the Father. Jesus is risen – he lives among us. We must listen to his presence and enter ever more deeply into the life of love of the Holy Trinity.

Personal Exercise
Spend some time reflecting on the truth that the Word of God is comprised both of sacred scripture and sacred tradition.

Lenten Prayer
Let us pray for the courage to nurture and nourish our faith life through attentiveness to the presence of Jesus revealed in word and sacrament.
We ask this through Christ our Lord. Amen.

The apostles said to the Lord, 'Increase our faith'. *Luke 17:5*

FIRST WEEK OF LENT: FRIDAY

Jesus casts out all fear

A reading from the holy Gospel according to Matthew
When they heard this, the disciples fell on their faces, overcome with fear. But Jesus came up and touched them. 'Stand up,' he said, 'do not be afraid.' And when they raised their eyes they saw no one but only Jesus.

As they came down from the mountain Jesus gave them this order. 'Tell no one about the vision until the Son of Man has risen from the dead.'

Jesus comes to them in their fear
The disciples' response to the vision of the Transfiguration is one of fear. This shows that it is not altogether uncommon for fear to be felt when God reveals his presence. The good news is that in such times Jesus himself comes to his followers and helps them to get back on their feet. Jesus casts out all fear by revealing his presence as that of total love.

Personal Exercise
Try to become more docile to the movement of the Holy Spirit within you as you engage in praying to God's Word, Jesus Christ.

Lenten Prayer
Let us pray for the ability to live in faith through remembering that Father, Son, and Holy Spirit continually call us to newness of life.
We ask this through Christ our Lord. Amen.

Stay firm in the faith. *1 Corinthians 16:13*

GROUP MEETING BEFORE THE SECOND SUNDAY

Gathering as the tiny Church.
Some moments of relaxation and becoming quiet.
Proclamation of the Word of God: Readings for the Second Sunday of Lent.

Questions for sharing in dialogue
The journey of faith calls us ever to conversion and growth in the love of God shown through the death and resurrection of Jesus. Our natural inclination seems to be to stay put and to settle for comfort. How do you feel about the constant demand made of you by God's love? How afraid are you of change? How often do you ask Jesus to help you change for the better?
Relaxing music to be played as questions are reflected upon to allow you to find meaning through, with, and in the Word of God.

From dialogue to praise
Once stories and any relevant dialogue have been shared the person leading the session says: We have heard the Word of God announce that there is no need for us to be afraid. We need have no fear for Jesus is with us.

Liturgical Memory
As we continue our journey through Lent we remember we share in the glory of God through our relationship with the risen Jesus. We clothe ourselves with the love which dispels all fear as we contemplate the words of our Lenten liturgy:

> Father, all-powerful and ever-living God,
> we do well always and everywhere to give you thanks
> through Jesus Christ our Lord.
> On your holy mountain he revealed himself in glory
> in the presence of his disciples.
> He had already prepared them for his approaching death.
> He wanted to teach them through the Law and the Prophets
> that the promised Christ had first to suffer
> and so come to the glory of his resurrection.
> In our unending joy we echo on earth the song of the angels

in heaven as they praise your glory for ever:
Holy, holy, holy ...

Living Word
Remembering the gift of the Son that the Father has given to us we listen attentively to his voice: Do not be afraid.

(Name), Jesus speaks these words to you:
Do not be afraid.

Quiet time/ Intercessions

Closing Prayer
Let us pray with confidence using the words of Jesus: Our Father ...

Blessing
Lord, bless and strengthen your people.
May they remain faithful to you
and always rejoice in your mercy.
We ask this in the name of Jesus the Lord. Amen.

The Lord grant us a quiet night and a perfect end. Amen.

A reading from the book of Genesis
Abraham is called by God.

The Lord said to Abram, 'Leave your country, your family and your father's house, for the land I will show you. I will make you a great nation; I will bless you and make your name so famous that it will be used as a blessing. I will bless those who bless you: I will curse those who slight you. All the tribes of the earth shall bless themselves by you.' So Abram went as the Lord told him.
This is the word of the Lord.

Responsorial Psalm
Response: May your love be upon us, O Lord,
    as we place all our hope in you.

> The word of the Lord is faithful
> and all his works to be trusted.
> The Lord loves justice and right
> and fills the earth with his love. R.

> The Lord looks on those who revere him,
> on those who hope in his love,
> to rescue their souls from death,
> to keep them alive in famine. R.

> Our soul is waiting for the Lord.
> The Lord is our help and our shield.
> May your love be upon us, O Lord,
> as we place all our hope in you. R.

A reading from the letter of St Paul to Timothy
Rely on the power of God revealed to us in the risen Lord.

With me, bear the hardships for the sake of the good news, relying on the power of God who has saved us and called us to be holy – not because of anything we ourselves have done but for his own purposes and by his own grace. This grace had already been granted to us, in Christ Jesus, before the beginning of time,

but it has only been revealed by the Appearing of our saviour Christ Jesus. He abolished death, and he has proclaimed life and immortality through the good news.
This is the word of the Lord.

Glory and praise to you, O Christ!
From the bright cloud the Father's voice was heard:
'This is my Son, the Beloved. Listen to him!'
Glory and praise to you, O Christ!

A reading from the holy Gospel according to Matthew
Jesus is transfigured on the high mountain

Jesus took with him Peter and James and his brother John and led them up a high mountain where they could be alone. There in their presence he was transfigured; his face shone like the sun and his clothes became as white as the light.

Suddenly Moses and Elijah appeared to them; they were talking with him. Then Peter spoke to Jesus. 'Lord,' he said 'it is wonderful for us to be here; if you wish, I will make three tents here, one for you, one for Moses and one for Elijah.'

He was still speaking when suddenly a bright cloud covered them with shadow, and from the cloud there came a voice which said, 'This is my Son, the Beloved; he enjoys my favour. Listen to him.'

When they heard this, the disciples fell on their faces, overcome with fear. But Jesus came up and touched them. 'Stand up,' he said, 'do not be afraid.' And when they raised their eyes they saw no one but only Jesus.

As they came down from the mountain Jesus gave them this order. 'Tell no one about the vision until the Son of Man has risen from the dead.'
This is the Gospel of the Lord.

Jesus is the Water of Life

A reading from the book of Exodus
Tormented by thirst, the people complained against Moses. 'Why did you bring us out of Egypt?' they said. 'Was it so that I should die of thirst, my children too, and my cattle?' Moses appealed to the Lord. 'How am I to deal with this people?' he said. 'A little more and they will stone me!' The Lord said to Moses, 'Take with you some of the elders of Israel and move on to the forefront of the people; take in your hand the staff with which you struck the river, and go. I shall be standing before you there on the rock, at Horeb. You must strike the rock, and water will flow from it for the people to drink.'

Water from the rock
When the people complained to Moses, Moses complained to God, and God worked the miracle of bringing forth flowing water from rock. The living God has the power to bring forth torrents of new life from places that seem all but barren to our human ways of thinking. God never gives up on anyone. God is the God of Life who calls all people to live life to the full.

Personal Exercise
Bring to Jesus the areas of your life where you have hardened your heart and ask him to soften them through, with, and in the Spirit of Love.

Lenten Prayer
Let us pray for the strength and courage to face any places of hardness within us and allow the love of God to draw forth water from such rock.
We ask this through Christ our Lord. Amen.

I will pour out water on the thirsty soil. *Isaiah 44:3*

Jesus is the Water of Life

A reading from the book of Psalms
Come, ring out our joy to the Lord; hail the rock who saves us.
Let us come before him, giving thanks,
with songs let us hail the Lord.

Come in; let us bow and bend low; let us kneel before the God who made us for he is our God and we the people who belong to his pasture, the flock that is led by his hand.

O that today you would listen to his voice! 'Harden not your hearts as at Meribah, as on that day at Massah in the desert when your fathers put me to the test; when they tried me, though they saw my work.'

Give joy to the Lord
In the psalm the writer remembers the incident from the time of Moses where God brought forth the water from the rock. For us Jesus is the Water of Life whom God brings forth to nurture and nourish our life of faith that flows from the Father, the Son, and the Holy Spirit.

Personal Exercise
Try to become gentler by relating to yourself and your limitations through awakening and remembering with joy God's love for you in Christ Jesus.

Lenten Prayer
Let us pray to be more confident in God's love revealed through Jesus so as to overcome our human weakness.
We ask this through Christ our Lord. Amen.

Come to the water all you who are thirsty. *Isaiah 55:1*

Jesus is the Water of Life

A reading from the letter of St Paul to the Romans
Through our Lord Jesus Christ by faith we are judged righteous and at peace with God, since it is by faith and through Jesus that we have entered this state of grace in which we can boast about looking forward to God's glory. This hope is not deceptive, because the love of God has been poured into our hearts by the Holy Spirit which has been given us. We were still helpless when at his appointed moment Christ died for sinful men. It is not easy to die even for a good man – though of course for someone really worthy, a man might be prepared to die – but what proves that God loves us is that Christ died for us while we were sinners.

The Holy Spirit is given to us
Through our faith in Christ the Holy Spirit has been poured into our heart. This gift of being made into an adopted child of God allows us also to enjoy the gift of Christ's peace. The Holy Spirit of Jesus is the water of God's life in us. It is this Holy Spirit that is continually moulding and guiding our thoughts, feelings, and actions so as to enable us to grow in the eternal life of the Holy Trinity.

Personal Exercise
Become more aware of the Holy Spirit prompting you to make acts of love in thought, word, and deed.

Lenten Prayer
Let us pray for the grace to understand more deeply how the Holy Spirit waters the garden of our inner life.
We ask this through Christ our Lord. Amen.

All who want it may have the water of life. *Revelations 22:17*

SECOND WEEK OF LENT: THURSDAY

Jesus is the Water of Life

A reading from the holy Gospel according to John
Jesus came to the Samaritan town called Sychar, near the land that Jacob gave to his son Joseph. Jacob's well is there and Jesus, tired by the journey, sat straight down by the well. It was about the sixth hour. When a Samaritan woman came to draw water, Jesus said to her, 'Give me a drink.' His disciples had gone into town to buy food. The Samaritan woman said to him, 'What? You are a Jew and you ask me, a Samaritan, for a drink?' – Jews, in fact, do not associate with Samaritans. Jesus replied: 'If you only knew what God is offering and who it is that is saying to you: Give me a drink, you would have been the one to ask, and he would have given you living water.'

God in Christ offers the living water of the Holy Spirit
The Samaritan woman does not realise who Jesus is or what he is capable of offering her in the name of the living God. In some ways she perhaps mirrors us who sometimes forget the marvel of the new life God offers us through the waters of our baptism. How often do we think about or thank God for the gift of faith we have received in the name of the Father, the Son, and the Holy Spirit?

Personal Exercise
Spend some time thinking about what it means for you to have been baptised into the life of the living God – Father, Son, and Holy Spirit.

Lenten Prayer
Let us pray for the ability to thank God for the many gifts he has given us – especially the gift of being baptised into the life of the Trinity.
We ask this through Christ our Lord. Amen.

I baptise you in water. *Matthew 3:11*

Jesus is the Water of Life

A reading from the holy Gospel according to John
Jesus replied: 'Whoever drinks this water will get thirsty again; but anyone who drinks the water that I shall give will never be thirsty again: the water that I shall give will turn into a spring inside him, welling up to eternal life.'

Life in the Holy Spirit
Jesus speaks of the difference between the physical reality of water quenching thirst and the life to be lived in the Holy Spirit – understood through using the symbol of a living spring of water. The good news for us is we have the promise of Jesus that if we cherish and look after the gift of the Holy Spirit poured into our heart through the waters of baptism then this life will grow and develop to the point where we will possess eternal life.

Personal Exercise
Reflect on how much you give witness to the life of the Holy Spirit that has been poured into your heart.

Lenten Prayer
Let us pray to be ever more convinced that God wishes to give the water of life of the Holy Spirit to all those who want it.
We ask this through Christ our Lord. Amen.

God's rivers brim with water. *Psalm 65:9*

GROUP MEETING BEFORE THE THIRD SUNDAY

Gathering as the tiny Church.
Some moments of relaxation and becoming quiet.
Proclamation of the Word of God: Readings for the Third Sunday of Lent.

Questions for sharing in dialogue
We turn our minds and hearts towards the mystery of the Holy Spirit of Jesus described for us as the living water. What areas of your life need to be watered by the Holy Spirit to awaken new meaning in Christ? In what ways does the Holy Spirit influence your thoughts, feelings and actions? How can you be more open to the influence of the Holy Spirit?
Relaxing music to be played as questions are reflected upon to allow you to find meaning through, with, and in the Word of God.

From dialogue to praise
Once stories and any relevant dialogue have been shared the person leading the session says: We remember the evidence God gives us of his Son's resurrection is that we share in the life of the Trinity through the gift of the Holy Spirit poured into our heart. The Holy Spirit waters the garden of our inner life through our sharing in the life of God's Son.

Liturgical Memory
During this season of Lent we bring to mind our need for the Holy Spirit to awaken once more in us the desire to drink from the fountain of living water, and to find the true meaning of our lives through, with, and in the risen Lord. With this in mind we recall the words of our Lenten liturgy:

> Father, all-powerful and ever-living God,
> we do well always and everywhere to give you thanks
> through Jesus Christ our Lord.
> When he asked the woman of Samaria for water to drink
> Christ had already prepared for her the gift of faith.
> In his thirst to receive her faith
> he awakened in her heart the fire of your love.

With thankful praise, in company with the angels,
We glorify the wonders of your power:
Holy, holy, holy ...

Living Word
We remember the words of Jesus who is the living wisdom of God: Anyone who drinks the water I shall give will never be thirsty.

(Name), Jesus speaks these words to you:
Anyone who drinks the water I shall give will never be thirsty.

Quiet time/ Intercessions

Closing Prayer
Let us ask our Father to forgive our sins and to bring us to forgive those who sin against us: Our Father ...

Blessing
Lord, may all Christian people both know and cherish
the heavenly gifts they have received.
We ask this in the name of Jesus the Lord. Amen.

The Lord grant us a quiet night and a perfect end. Amen.

A reading from the book of Exodus
Water flows from the rock.
Tormented by thirst, the people complained against Moses. 'Why did you bring us out of Egypt?' they said. 'Was it so that I should die of thirst, my children too, and my cattle?' Moses appealed to the Lord. 'How am I to deal with this people?' he said. 'A little more and they will stone me!' The Lord said to Moses, 'Take with you some of the elders of Israel and move on to the forefront of the people; take in your hand the staff with which you struck the river, and go. I shall be standing before you there on the rock, at Horeb. You must strike the rock, and water will flow from it for the people to drink.' This is what Moses did, in the sight of the elders of Israel. The place was named Massah and Meribah because of the grumbling of the sons of Israel and because they put the Lord to the test by saying, 'Is the Lord with us, or not?'
This is the word of the Lord.

Responsorial Psalm
Response: O that today you would listen to his voice:
  'Harden not your hearts.'

  Come, ring out our joy to the Lord; hail the rock who saves us.
  Let us come before him, giving thanks,
  with songs let us hail the Lord. R.

  Come in; let us bow and bend low; let us kneel before the God who made us for he is our God and we the people who belong to his pasture, the flock that is led by his hand. R.

  O that today you would listen to his voice! 'Harden not your hearts as at Meribah, as on that day at Massah in the desert when your fathers put me to the test; when they tried me, though they saw my work.' R.

A reading from the first letter of St Paul to the Romans.
Christ died for us whilst we were yet sinners.

Through our Lord Jesus Christ by faith we are judged righteous and at peace with God, since it is by faith and through Jesus that we have entered this state of grace in which we can boast about looking forward to God's glory. This hope is not deceptive, because the love of God has been poured into our hearts by the Holy Spirit which has been given us. We were still helpless when at his appointed moment Christ died for sinful men. It is not easy to die even for a good man – though of course for someone really worthy, a man might be prepared to die – but what proves that God loves us is that Christ died for us while we were sinners.
This is the word of the Lord.

Glory to you, O Christ, you are the Word of God!
Lord, you are really the saviour of the world;
give me the living water, so that I may never get thirsty.
Glory to you, O Christ, you are the Word of God!

A reading from the holy Gospel according to John
The risen Jesus gives us the living water of the Holy Spirit.

Jesus came to the Samaritan town called Sychar, near the land that Jacob gave to his son Joseph. Jacob's well is there and Jesus, tired by the journey, sat straight down by the well. It was about the sixth hour. When a Samaritan woman came to draw water, Jesus said to her, 'Give me a drink.' His disciples had gone into town to buy food. The Samaritan woman said to him, 'What? You are a Jew and you ask me, a Samaritan, for a drink?' – Jews, in fact, do not associate with Samaritans. Jesus replied: 'If you only knew what God is offering and who it is that is saying to you: Give me a drink, you would have been the one to ask, and he would have given you living water.' 'You have no bucket, sir,' she answered, 'and the well is deep: how could you get this living water? Are you a greater man than our father Jacob who gave us this well and drank from it himself with his sons and his cattle?'

Jesus replied: 'Whoever drinks this water will get thirsty again; but anyone who drinks the water that I shall give will never be thirsty again: the water that I shall give will turn into a spring inside him, welling up to eternal life.' 'Sir,' said the woman, 'give me some of that water, so that I may never get thirsty and never have to come here again to draw water. I see you are a prophet, sir,' said the woman. 'Our fathers worshipped on this mountain, while you say that Jerusalem is the place where one ought to worship.'

Jesus said: 'Believe me, woman, the hour is coming when you will worship the Father neither on this mountain nor in Jerusalem. You worship what you do not know; we worship what we do know; for salvation comes from the Jews. But the hour will come – in fact it is here already – when true worshippers will worship the Father in spirit and truth: that is the kind of worshipper the Father wants. God is spirit, and those who worship must worship in spirit and truth.

The woman said to him, 'I know the Messiah – that is, Christ – is coming; and when he comes he will tell us everything.' 'I who am speaking to you,' said Jesus 'I am he.'

Many Samaritans of that town had believed in him on the strength of the woman's testimony when she said, 'He told me all I have ever done,' so when the Samaritans came up to him, they begged him to stay with them. He stayed for two days, and when he spoke to them many more came to believe; and they said to the woman, 'Now we no longer believe because of what you told us; we have heard him ourselves and we know that he really is the saviour of the world.'

This is the Gospel of the Lord.

Jesus gives us eyes of faith

A reading from the first book of Samuel
Jesse presented his seven sons to Samuel, but Samuel said to Jesse, 'The Lord has not chosen these.' He answered, 'There is still one left, the youngest; he is out looking after the sheep.' Then Samuel said to Jesse, 'Send for him; we will not sit down to eat until he comes.' Jesse had him sent for, a boy of fresh complexion, with fine eyes and pleasant bearing. The Lord said, 'Come, anoint him, for this is the one.' At this, Samuel took the horn of oil and anointed him where he stood with his brothers; and the spirit of the Lord seized on David and stayed with him from that day on.

The Lord chooses David
The Lord chose David from the sons of Jesse to be a king. The Lord's choice was surprising to both Samuel and Jesse because they were assessing the sons by appearance and height and not in the same manner as the Lord – by what is in a person's heart.

To look beyond the physical to the spiritual, from the cover to the content, is to learn how to see with the same eyes as the Lord. It is to begin to see with the eyes of faith.

Personal Exercise
Spend some time reflecting on how you use the gift of faith given you by God the Father, Son, and Holy Spirit.

Lenten Prayer
Let us pray that the faith and love we already possess will increase through our responding in integrity to the revelation of God's love revealed in Christ Jesus.
We ask this through Christ our Lord. Amen.

Where is your faith? *Luke 8:25*

THIRD WEEK OF LENT: TUESDAY

Jesus gives us eyes of faith

A reading from the book of Psalms
The Lord is my shepherd; there is nothing I shall want.
Fresh and green are the pastures where he gives me repose.
Near restful water he leads me to revive my drooping spirit.
He guides me along the right path; he is true to his name.
If I should walk in the valley of darkness no evil would I fear.
You are there with your crook and your staff;
with these you give me comfort.
You have prepared a banquet for me in the sight of my foes.
My head you have anointed with oil; my cup is overflowing.
Surely goodness and kindness shall follow me all the days of my life.
In the Lord's own house shall I dwell for ever and ever.

The Lord is my shepherd
When we awaken our faith and use it to understand and interpret our lives we realise the Lord himself is a personal shepherd who looks after us and guides us.

Personal Exercise
Pray for the grace to remember to awaken the gift of your faith as often as possible.

Lenten Prayer
Let us pray for the ability to live and act in a universe of love through awakening and remembering our faith in the risen Lord.
We ask this through Christ our Lord. Amen.

What matters is faith that makes its power felt through love.
Galatians 5:6

Jesus gives us eyes of faith

A reading from the letter to the Ephesians
You were darkness once, but now you are light in the Lord; be like children of light, for the effects of the light are seen in complete goodness and right living and truth. Try to discover what the Lord wants of you, having nothing to do with the futile works of darkness but exposing them by contrast. The things which are done in secret are things that people are ashamed even to speak of; but anything exposed by the light will be illuminated and anything illuminated turns into light. That is why it is said: Wake up from your sleep, rise from the dead, and Christ will shine on you.

We live in the light of the Lord
The risen Lord urges us to wake up from the state of being spiritually asleep. We have his promise that he will shine his light on our minds and hearts to illuminate and guide our way. This is how we 'rise from the dead' and live lives of resurrection faith. This is how we 'see' with the eyes of faith.

Personal Exercise
Show your faith in Christ through some form of loving action today.

Lenten Prayer
Let us pray for the courage to awaken and show forth our faith in Jesus through revealing its power in loving action.
We ask this through Christ our Lord. Amen.

Christ may live in your hearts through faith. *Ephesians 3:17*

THIRD WEEK OF LENT: THURSDAY

Jesus gives us eyes of faith

A reading from the holy Gospel according to John
They brought the man who had been blind to the Pharisees. It had been a sabbath day when Jesus made the paste and opened the man's eyes, so when the Pharisees asked him how he had come to see, he said, 'He put a paste on my eyes, and I washed, and I can see.' Then some of the Pharisees said, 'This man cannot be from God: he does not keep the sabbath.' Others said, 'How could a sinner produce signs like this?' And there was disagreement among them, so they spoke to the blind man again, 'What have you to say about him yourself, now that he has opened your eyes?' 'He is a prophet' replied the man.

What have you to say?
The Pharisees decide to pass judgement on Jesus by finding out what he did to allow the blind man to see. They eventually come to ask the man himself what he has to say about Jesus. We are in a similar position to the man in the sense that we have been given the gift of having faith in the person of the risen Jesus which allows us to see our lives in a different light. When questioned by those who have not yet met Jesus we too must be ready to answer the question: 'What have you to say about him yourself?'

Personal Exercise
Spend some time reflecting on your relationship with the risen Lord so you can answer the question 'What have you to say about him yourself?'

Lenten Prayer
Let us pray for the gift to see with the eyes of faith and so understand and interpret our existence in relation to the risen Lord. We ask this through Christ our Lord. Amen.

You have great faith. *Matthew 15:28*

Jesus gives us eyes of faith

A reading from the holy Gospel according to John
Jesus heard they had driven the man who had been blind away, and when he found him he said to him, 'Do you believe in the Son of Man?' 'Sir,' the man replied, 'tell me who he is so that I may believe in him.' Jesus said, 'You are looking at him; he is speaking to you.' The man said, 'Lord, I believe', and worshipped him.

Jesus seeks the man he cured
Jesus goes in search of the man who had been blind to bring his faith to fruition. Jesus has led the man from the darkness of having no faith to the light of worshipping the living God with living faith. We too must learn to awaken our living faith in the risen Lord so as to give him glory and praise each and every day through the living offering of our lives.

Personal Exercise
Try to see your world through the eyes of faith and love given as a gift by Christ Jesus.

Lenten Prayer
Let us pray that this Lent we will grow in our desire to give glory and praise to the God of the Holy Trinity.
We ask this through Christ our Lord. Amen.

Only faith can guarantee the blessing that we hope for.
Hebrews 11:1.

GROUP MEETING BEFORE THE FOURTH SUNDAY

Gathering as the tiny church.
Some moments of relaxation and becoming quiet.
Proclamation of the Word of God: Readings for the Fourth Sunday of Lent.

Questions for sharing in dialogue
Our focus is to awaken and use our eyes of faith to understand and interpret our lives as followers of the risen Jesus. To what extent do you remember to awaken the gift of your faith on a daily basis? How easy/difficult do you find it to see your life through the eyes of faith? In what ways does your faith in Jesus bring meaning to your life?
Relaxing music to be played as questions are reflected upon to allow you to find meaning through, with, and in the Word of God.

From dialogue to praise
Once stories and any relevant dialogue have been shared the person leading the session says: Together we have remembered how much we believe in the risen Lord and dedicate ourselves to him. We give thanks to the living God for the gift of our faith.

Liturgical Memory
Remembering it is the risen Lord who opens our eyes to teach us his way and walk by his light, we recall the words the priest prays on our behalf at this time of Lent:
    Father, all-powerful and ever-living God,
      we do well always and everywhere to give you thanks
      through Jesus Christ our Lord.
    He came among us as a man,
      to lead humanity from darkness into the light of faith.
    Through Adam's fall we were born as slaves of sin,
      but now through baptism in Christ
    we are reborn as your adopted children.
    Earth unites with heaven to sing the new song of creation,
      as we adore and praise you for ever:
    Holy, holy, holy ...

Living Word
The risen Lord is always with us and wishes us to grow in the way of his love. He gives us the choice once more to say yes to him and so he asks of us: Do you believe?

(Name), Jesus speaks these words to you:
Do you believe?

Quiet time/ Intercessions

Closing Prayer
Let us pray for the coming of the kingdom as Jesus taught us:
Our Father ...

Blessing
Lord, we pray for your people who believe in you.
May they enjoy the gift of your love, share it with others,
and spread it everywhere.
We ask this in the name of Jesus the Lord. Amen.

The Lord grant us a quiet night and a perfect end. Amen.

A reading from the first book of Samuel
David is anointed king of Israel.

The Lord said to Samuel, 'Fill your horn with oil and go. I am sending you to Jesse of Bethlehem, for I have chosen myself a king among his sons.' When Samuel arrived he caught sight of Eliab and thought, 'Surely the Lord's anointed one stands there before him,' but the Lord said to Samuel, 'Take no notice of his appearance or his height for I have rejected him; God does not see as man sees; man looks at appearances but the Lord looks at the heart.'

Jesse presented his seven sons to Samuel, but Samuel said to Jesse, 'The Lord has not chosen these.' He answered, 'There is still one left, the youngest; he is out looking after the sheep.' Then Samuel said to Jesse, 'Send for him; we will not sit down to eat until he comes.' Jesse had him sent for, a boy of fresh complexion, with fine eyes and pleasant bearing. The Lord said, 'Come, anoint him, for this is the one.' At this, Samuel took the horn of oil and anointed him where he stood with his brothers; and the spirit of the Lord seized on David and stayed with him from that day on.
This is the word of the Lord.

Responsorial Psalm
Response: The Lord is my shepherd; there is nothing I shall want.

The Lord is my shepherd; there is nothing I shall want.
Fresh and green are the pastures where he gives me repose.
Near restful water he leads me to revive my drooping spirit. *R.*

He guides me along the right path; he is true to his name.
If I should walk in the valley of darkness no evil would I fear.
You are there with your crook and your staff;
with these you give me comfort. *R.*

You have prepared a banquet for me in the sight of my foes.
My head you have anointed with oil; my cup is overflowing. *R.*

Surely goodness and kindness shall follow me
all the days of my life.
In the Lord's own house shall I dwell for ever and ever. R.

A reading from the letter to the Ephesians
Be like children of light.

You were darkness once, but now you are light in the Lord; be like children of light, for the effects of the light are seen in complete goodness and right living and truth. Try to discover what the Lord wants of you, having nothing to do with the futile works of darkness but exposing them by contrast. The things which are done in secret are things that people are ashamed even to speak of; but anything exposed by the light will be illuminated and anything illuminated turns into light. That is why it is said: Wake up from your sleep, rise from the dead, and Christ will shine on you.
This is the word of the Lord.

Glory to you, O Christ, you are the Word of God!
I am the light of the world, says the Lord;
anyone who follows me will have the light of life.
Glory to you, O Christ, you are the Word of God!

A reading from the holy Gospel according to John
Jesus gives sight to the man born blind.

As Jesus went along, he saw a man who had been blind from birth. He spat on the ground, made a paste with the spittle, put this over the eyes of the blind man and said to him, 'Go and wash in the Pool of Siloam' (a name that means 'sent'). So the blind man went off and washed himself, and came away with his sight restored.

His neighbours and people who earlier had seen him begging said, 'Isn't this the man who used to sit and beg?' Some said, 'Yes, it is the same one.' Others said, 'No, he only looks like him.' The man himself said, 'I am the man.'

They brought the man who had been blind to the Pharisees. It had been a sabbath day when Jesus made the paste and opened the man's eyes, so when the Pharisees asked him how he had come to see, he said, 'He put a paste on my eyes, and I washed, and I can see.' Then some of the Pharisees said, 'This man cannot be from God: he does not keep the sabbath.' Others said, 'How could a sinner produce signs like this?' And there was disagreement among them, so they spoke to the blind man again, 'What have you to say about him yourself, now that he has opened your eyes?' 'He is a prophet' replied the man.

'Are you trying to teach us' they replied 'and you a sinner through and through, since you were born!' And they drove him away.

Jesus heard they had driven him away, and when he found him he said to him, 'Do you believe in the Son of Man?' 'Sir,' the man replied, 'tell me who he is so that I may believe in him.' Jesus said, 'You are looking at him; he is speaking to you.' The man said, 'Lord, I believe', and worshipped him.

This is the Gospel of the Lord.

Life in the Spirit of Jesus

A reading from the prophet Ezekiel
The Lord says this: 'I am now going to open your graves; I mean to raise you from your graves, my people, and lead you back to the soil of Israel. And you will know that I am the Lord, when I open your graves and raise you from your graves, my people. And I shall put my spirit in you, and you will live, and I shall resettle you on your own soil; and you will know that I, the Lord, have said and done this – it is the Lord who speaks.'

God's Spirit gives us life
It is the risen Lord who opens up those areas of our lives which we have closed off because we have settled for death. Only he can bring life to the graves that live inside us because it is only through the power of love that these areas can be opened up and transformed to yield life. Such areas may be memories of hurt, broken relationships, a lack of self-confidence or self-respect etc. The life that arises is the life that comes through living in relationship with the Spirit of the Lord. He has the power to heal us in love through the saving action of the Holy Spirit.

Personal Exercise
Invite the risen Lord to attend to those areas of your inner life where you want the Holy Spirit to bring new life.

Lenten Prayer
Let us pray for the grace to understand that true freedom is found only through living in relationship with the Spirit of the Lord. We ask this through Christ our Lord. Amen.

Anyone who is joined to the Lord is one spirit with him.
1 Corinthians 6:17

Life in the Spirit of Jesus

A reading from the letter of St Paul to the Romans
People who are interested only in unspiritual things can never be pleasing to God. Your interests, however, are not in the unspiritual, but in the spiritual, since the Spirit of God has made his home in you. In fact, unless you possessed the Spirit of Christ you would not belong to him. Though your body may be dead it is because of sin, but if Christ is in you then your spirit is life itself because you have been justified; and if the Spirit of him who raised Jesus from the dead is living in you, then he who raised Jesus from the dead will give life to your own mortal bodies through his Spirit living in you.

The Spirit of Christ lives in us
We belong to Christ because we possess his Spirit through our baptism. It is this Spirit of Christ that lives in us and gives life not only to our spiritual lives but also to our mortal bodies. We have the responsibility to cultivate interest in our life in the Spirit because it is through such nurture and nourishment that we will grow more and more in the love of God revealed in the passion, death and resurrection of Jesus.

Personal Exercise
Pay a deeper attention than usual to your inner life, becoming more aware of how the Holy Spirit influences your thoughts, feelings, and actions.

Lenten Prayer
Let us pray for the grace to pay more attention to the working of the Holy Spirit in our lives.
We ask this through Christ our Lord. Amen.

The Spirit is our life. *Galatians 5:25*

Life in the Spirit of Jesus

A reading from the holy Gospel according to John
When Martha heard that Jesus had come she went to meet him. Mary remained sitting in the house. Martha said to Jesus, 'If you had been here, my brother would not have died, but I know that, even now, whatever you ask of God, he will grant you.'

Jesus is our way to God
We are in the same situation as Martha in our relationship with Jesus. We know that whatever Jesus asks of God it will be granted. However, the gifts that are to be granted are gifts in the realm of the life-giving Spirit. Our prayer then is to be directed primarily to respect this truth of our life in God.

Personal Exercise
Pray for a person other than yourself, that they will receive a fresh outpouring of the Holy Spirit in their mind and heart.

Lenten Prayer
Let us pray for the grace to remember what the Spirit of Jesus can do for us.
We ask this through Christ our Lord. Amen.

Be filled with the Spirit. *Ephesians 5:18*

Life in the Spirit of Jesus

A reading from the holy Gospel according to John
Jesus said: 'I am the resurrection and the life. If anyone believes in me, even though he dies he will live, and whoever lives and believes in me will never die. Do you believe this?' 'Yes Lord,' she said 'I believe that you are the Christ, the Son of God, the one who was to come into the world.'

Jesus said in great distress, with a sigh that came straight from the heart, 'Where have you put him?' They said, 'Lord, come and see.' Jesus wept; and the Jews said, 'See how much he loved him!'

Jesus shows his love for Lazarus
Jesus is not afraid to show his love for Lazarus. He sheds tears on the event of the death of his friend. However, because Jesus is the resurrection and the life he can bring life to Lazarus even although he lies dead in the tomb. As the risen Lord, Jesus is the resurrection and the life for us. The way he raises us from the dead is by pouring the Holy Spirit into our hearts so as to lead us to new life in him as we journey together to the Father.

Personal Exercise
Bring new life to a person whom you love today and show the Holy Spirit is at work in your life.

Lenten Prayer
Let us pray for the grace to become more like Christ.
We ask this through Christ our Lord. Amen.

Let us be directed by the Spirit. *Galatians 5:25*

Life in the Spirit of Jesus

A reading from the holy Gospel according to John
Jesus said, 'Take the stone away.' Martha said to him 'Lord by now he will smell; this is the fourth day.' Jesus replied 'Have I not told you that if you believe you will see the glory of God?' So they took away the stone. Then Jesus lifted up his eyes and said: 'Father, I thank you for hearing my prayer. I knew indeed that you always hear me. But I speak for the sake of all these who stand round me, so that they may believe it was you who sent me.'

When he had said this, he cried out in a loud voice, 'Lazarus, here! Come out!' The dead man came out, his feet and hands bound with bands of stuff and a cloth round his face. Jesus said to them, 'Unbind him, let him go free.' Many of the Jews who had come to visit Mary and had seen what he did believed in him.

Jesus reveals the glory of God
Jesus raises Lazarus from the dead so that God the Father may be glorified. We are to continue this mission of Jesus by living in accord with the gift of the Holy Spirit and so ensure people come to give glory and service to God inspired by the example of our lives.

Personal Exercise
Enjoy the truth that through your baptism you bear the fruits of the Spirit in your life as an example to all who seek the God of love.

Lenten Prayer
Let us pray for the grace never to suppress the Spirit at work among us bearing the spiritual fruit we need.
We ask this through Christ our Lord. Amen.

Never try to suppress the Spirit. *1 Thessalonians 5:19*

GROUP MEETING BEFORE THE FIFTH SUNDAY

Gathering as the tiny church.
Some moments of relaxation and becoming quiet.
Proclamation of the Word of God: Readings for the Fifth Sunday of Lent.

Questions for sharing in dialogue
Jesus wept at the death of his friend Lazarus and showed the depth of his love. How much do you feel loved by Jesus? What do you do to stay in touch with God's love for you? As a Christian, how do you stay open to the Spirit of Jesus, the Spirit of Love in your life?
Relaxing music to be played as questions are reflected upon to allow you to find meaning through, with, and in the Word of God.

From dialogue to praise
Once stories and any relevant dialogue have been shared the person leading the session says: We have shared how much the love of the risen Jesus influences our lives. We have revealed to one another that the Spirit of Christ lives in our minds and hearts and that he is the resurrection and our life.

Liturgical Memory
During this Lenten time we call to mind the depth of God's love revealed in the person of Jesus who is fully God and fully human. In our Lenten liturgy we remember how Jesus was moved to tears by the death of Lazarus:

> Father, all-powerful and ever-living God,
> we do well always and everywhere to give you thanks
> through Jesus Christ our Lord.
> As a man like us, Jesus wept for Lazarus his friend.
> As the eternal God, he raised Lazarus from the dead.
> In his love for us all, Christ gives us the sacraments
> to lift us up to everlasting life.
> Through him the angels of heaven offer their prayer
> of adoration as they rejoice in your presence for ever.

May our voices be one with theirs
in their triumphant hymn of praise: Holy, holy, holy ...

Living Word
As Christians our life in God is always through, with, and in the person of the risen Lord. With resurrection faith we hear him say to us in love: I am the resurrection and the life.

(Name), Jesus speaks these words to you:
I am the resurrection and the life.

Quiet time/ Intercessions

Closing Prayer
Let us pray for the coming of the kingdom as Jesus our friend and brother taught us: Our Father ...

Blessing
Lord, we ask for an increase in our faith.
May Jesus, the resurrection and the life, be known to others through our loving service of God and one another.
We ask this in the name of Jesus the Lord. Amen.

The Lord grant us a quiet night and a perfect end. Amen.

A reading from the prophet Ezekiel
I mean to raise you from your graves.

The Lord says this: I am now going to open your graves; I mean to raise you from your graves, my people, and lead you back to the soil of Israel. And you will know that I am the Lord, when I open your graves and raise you from your graves, my people. And I shall put my spirit in you, and you will live, and I shall resettle you on your own soil; and you will know that I, the Lord, have said and done this – it is the Lord who speaks.'
This is the word of the Lord.

Responsorial Psalm
Response: With the Lord there is mercy
and fullness of redemption.

Out of the depths I cry to you, O Lord,
Lord, hear my voice!
O let your ears be attentive
to the voice of my pleading. *R.*

If you, O Lord, should mark our guilt,
Lord, who would survive?
But with you is found forgiveness:
for this we revere you. *R.*

My soul is waiting for the Lord
I count on his word.
My soul is longing for the Lord
more than watchman for daybreak.
(Let the watchman count on daybreak
and Israel on the Lord.) *R.*

Because with the Lord there is mercy
and fullness of redemption.
Israel indeed he will redeem
from all its iniquity. *R.*

A reading from the letter of St Paul to the Romans
The Spirit of him who raised Jesus from the dead is living in you.

People who are interested only in unspiritual things can never be pleasing to God. Your interests, however, are not in the unspiritual, but in the spiritual, since the Spirit of God has made his home in you. In fact, unless you possessed the Spirit of Christ you would not belong to him. Though your body may be dead it is because of sin, but if Christ is in you then your spirit is life itself because you have been justified; and if the Spirit of him who raised Jesus from the dead is living in you, then he who raised Jesus from the dead will give life to your own mortal bodies through his Spirit living in you.
This is the word of the Lord.

Glory and praise to you, O Christ!
I am the resurrection and the life, says the Lord;
who ever believes in me will never die.
Glory and praise to you, O Christ!

A reading from the holy Gospel according to John
I am the resurrection and the life.

The sisters sent this message to Jesus, 'Lord, the man you love is ill.' On receiving the message, Jesus said, 'This sickness will end not in death but in God's glory, and through it the Son of God will be glorified.' Jesus loved Martha and her sister and Lazarus, yet when he heard that Lazarus was ill he stayed where he was for two more days before saying to his disciples, 'Let us go to Judaea.'

On arriving, Jesus found that Lazarus had been in the tomb for four days already. When Martha heard that Jesus had come she went to meet him. Mary remained sitting in the house. Martha said to Jesus, 'If you had been here, my brother would not have died, but I know that, even now, whatever you ask of God, he will grant you.' 'Your brother,' said Jesus to her, 'will rise again.' Martha said, 'I know he will rise again at the resurrection on the last day.' Jesus said: 'I am the resurrection and the life. If anyone believes in me, even though he dies he will live, and whoever lives and believes in me will never die. Do you believe this?' 'Yes Lord,' she said, 'I believe that you are the Christ, the Son of God, the one who was to come into the world.'

Jesus said in great distress, with a sigh that came straight from the heart, 'Where have you put him?' They said, 'Lord, come and see.' Jesus wept; and the Jews said, 'See how much he loved him!' But there were some who remarked, 'He opened the eyes of the blind man, could he not have prevented this man's death?'

Still sighing Jesus reached the tomb; it was a cave with a stone to close the opening. Jesus said, 'Take the stone away.' Martha said to him, 'Lord by now he will smell; this is the fourth day.' Jesus replied, 'Have I not told you that if you believe you will see the glory of God?' So they took away the stone. Then Jesus lifted up his eyes and said: 'Father, I thank you for hearing my prayer. I knew indeed that you always hear me. But I speak for the sake of all these who stand round me, so that they may believe it was you who sent me.'

When he had said this, he cried out in a loud voice, 'Lazarus, here! Come out!' The dead man came out, his feet and hands bound with bands of stuff and a cloth round his face. Jesus said to them, 'Unbind him, let him go free.' Many of the Jews who had come to visit Mary and had seen what he did believed in him.

This is the Gospel of the Lord.

Jesus reveals God's love for us

A reading from the prophet Isaiah
The Lord has given me a disciple's tongue. So that I may know how to reply to the wearied he provides me with speech. Each morning he wakes me to hear, to listen like a disciple. The Lord has opened my ear. For my part, I made no resistance, neither did I turn away. I offered my back to those who struck me, my cheeks to those who tore at my beard; I did not cover my face against insult and spittle. The Lord comes to my help, so that I am untouched by the insults. So, too, I set my face like flint; I know I shall not be shamed.

The Lord comes to help us
Isaiah understands his relationship with the Lord and his sense of God's activity in his life is as beautiful as it is wonderful. Like Isaiah we too are called to realise the presence and action of the risen Christ in our lives. Through clothing ourselves in Jesus we can face all of life's difficulties because we know he is always with us. The risen Christ is God's love for us. He is active and alive in our lives – not distant and removed.

Personal Exercise
Become more aware of how much you allow the living God of Jesus Christ to influence your decisions.

Lenten Prayer
Let us pray for a greater awareness and sensitivity towards the presence of the risen Lord at work in our lives.
We ask this through Christ our Lord. Amen.

Nothing can come between us and the love of Christ.
Romans 8:35

Jesus reveals God's love for us

A reading from the letter of St Paul to the Philippians
His state was divine, yet Christ Jesus did not cling to his equality with God but emptied himself to assume the condition of a slave, and became as men are, and being as all men are, he was humbler yet, even to accepting death, death on a cross.

But God raised him high and gave him the name which is above all other names so that all beings in the heavens, on earth and in the underworld, should bend the knee at the name of Jesus and that every tongue should acclaim Jesus Christ as Lord, to the glory of God the Father.

Jesus empties himself for us
God's love for us was shown when Jesus emptied himself to the point of death. To think that God in Christ humbled himself and died on the cross for us is more than our imagination can take – that is why it is a mystery of the heart. The love of God for us is the mystery of being overwhelmed in love by the person of the risen Lord.

Personal Exercise
Become more aware of how much you allow the love of God in Christ Jesus to influence your feelings and emotions.

Lenten Prayer
Let us pray for the docility of spirit to allow the love of Christ to overwhelm us.
We ask this through Christ our Lord. Amen.

The love of Christ overwhelms us. *2 Corinthians 5:14*

Jesus reveals God's love for us

A reading from the holy Gospel according to Matthew
Jesus was brought before Pontius Pilate, the governor, and the governor put to him this question, 'Are you the king of the Jews?' Jesus replied, 'It is you who say it.' But when he was accused by the chief priests and the elders he refused to answer at all. Pilate then said to him, 'Do you not hear how many charges they have brought against you?' But to the governor's complete amazement, he offered no reply to any of the charges.

The Passion of Jesus
The silence of Jesus is truly astounding. It shows such total lack of self-doubt that could only flow from his living relationship with Abba. Jesus knows full well that he is innocent. He does not need to defend himself. He thus puts the onus of proof on those who bring the charges against him. His silence thus becomes the mirror of truth for those who would manipulate and lie to bring about the death of God-made-man.

Personal Exercise
Become more aware of how you allow the example of Jesus Christ to influence your actions.

Lenten Prayer
Let us pray for the grace to meditate and learn from the example of Christ as he endures the passion for us.
We ask this through Christ our Lord. Amen.

God is love. *1 John 4:16*

Jesus reveals God's love for us

A reading from the holy Gospel according to Matthew
From the sixth hour there was darkness over all the land until the ninth hour. And about the ninth hour, Jesus cried out in a loud voice, 'Eli, Eli, lama sabachthani?' that is, 'My God, my God, why have you deserted me?' When some of those who stood there heard this, they said, 'The man is calling on Elijah,' and one of them quickly ran to get a sponge which he dipped in vinegar and, putting it on a reed, gave it him to drink. 'Wait!' said the rest of them, 'and see if Elijah will come to save him.' But Jesus, again crying out in a loud voice, yielded up his spirit.

The death of Jesus
Jesus has given his life so that each one of us could become an adopted child of God.

Personal Exercise
Spend some time today trying to touch the reality that God loves you so much that his only Son gave his life so that you could be adopted by God as a child whom he totally loves.

Lenten Prayer
Let us pray for a greater realisation of the price paid by Jesus to bring us into the life of the Holy Trinity.
We ask this through Christ our Lord. Amen.

God loved the world so much that he gave his only Son.
John 3:16

Jesus reveals God's love for us

A reading from the holy Gospel according to Matthew
At that, the veil of the Temple was torn in two from top to bottom; the earth quaked; the rocks were split; the tombs opened and the bodies of many holy men rose from the dead, and these, after his resurrection, came out of the tombs, entered the Holy City and appeared to a number of people. Meanwhile the centurion, together with the others guarding Jesus, had seen the earthquake and all that was taking place, and they were terrified and said, 'In truth this was a son of God.'

Jesus is revealed as God's Son
We are always to remember the story of the passion from the perspective of having living faith in the risen Jesus. As the greatest work of God's love for us, the passion reveals the depth of love God has for us now – through, with, and in the person of the risen Lord. As the Son of God, the risen Jesus loves us with an unconditional love.

Personal Exercise
Pray, by name, for all the people whom you love asking God to continue to pour the gift of the Spirit of Jesus into their hearts and minds.

Lenten Prayer
Let us pray for a greater realisation that our love for one another is grounded in and flows from God's love for us revealed in the passion, death, and resurrection of Jesus.
We ask this through Christ our Lord. Amen.

We are to love, then, because God loved us first. *1 John 4:19*

Gathering as the tiny church.
Some moments of relaxation and becoming quiet.
Proclamation of the Word of God: Readings for Passion Sunday.

Questions for sharing in dialogue
The passion of Jesus is the greatest revelation of God's love for us. Jesus gave his life so that we might become children of God. How often do you recall the love of God for you revealed through the death of Jesus? How do you allow yourself to be influenced by this love available to you through your relationship with the risen Lord? How does it feel to know the depth of God's love shown in the death and resurrection of Jesus?
Relaxing music to be played as questions are reflected upon to allow you to find meaning through, with, and in the Word of God.

From dialogue to praise
Once stories and any relevant dialogue have been shared the person leading the session says: We have shared how much the death and resurrection of the Lord means to us. Together, we have remembered the depth of God's love at work in our minds and hearts.

Liturgical Memory
In this holy season of Lent we have looked once more at our relationship with God in Christ and made ourselves open to the revelation of God's love for us shown in the dying and rising of Jesus. We remember the sacrifice Jesus made for us as we recall the words of our Lenten liturgy:
>Father, all-powerful and ever-living God,
>we do well always and everywhere to give you thanks,
>through Jesus Christ our Lord.
>Though he was sinless, he suffered willingly for sinners.
>Though innocent, he accepted death to save the guilty.
>By his dying, he has destroyed our sins.
>By his rising, he has raised us up to holiness of life.
>We praise you, Lord, with all the angels and saints
>in their song of joy: Holy, holy, holy ...

Living Word
The passion of Jesus reveals God's love for us. We must never forget that Jesus is both fully human and fully divine. Bearing this in mind we hear the risen Lord say: I am the son of God.

(Name), Jesus speaks these words to you: I am the son of God.

Quiet time/ Intercessions

Closing Prayer
Let us pray for the grace to open our hearts and minds to the depth of God's love for us revealed in the death and resurrection of his Son Jesus, as together we say: Our Father ...

Blessing
Lord, open our hearts and minds to your love for us.
We ask this in the name of Jesus the Lord. Amen.

The Lord grant us a quiet night and a perfect end. Amen.

READINGS FOR PASSION SUNDAY

A reading from the prophet Isaiah
The suffering servant of God.

The Lord has given me a disciple's tongue.
So that I may know how to reply to the wearied
he provides me with speech.
Each morning he wakes me to hear, to listen like a disciple.
The Lord has opened my ear.
For my part, I made no resistance, neither did I turn away.
I offered my back to those who struck me,
my cheeks to those who tore at my beard;
I did not cover my face against insult and spittle.
The Lord comes to my help,
so that I am untouched by the insults.
So, too, I set my face like flint; I know I shall not be shamed.
This is the word of the Lord.

Responsorial Psalm
Response: My God, my God, why have you forsaken me?

> All who see me deride me.
> They curl their lips, they toss their heads.
> 'He trusted in the Lord, let him save him;
> let him release him if this is his friend.' *R.*

> Many dogs have surrounded me,
> a band of the wicked beset me.
> They tear holes in my hands and my feet.
> I can count every one of my bones. *R.*

> They divide my clothing among them.
> They cast lots for my robe.
> O Lord, do not leave me alone,
> my strength, make haste to help me! *R.*

> I will tell of your name to my brethren
> and praise you where they are assembled.
> 'You who fear the Lord give him praise;
> all sons of Jacob, give him glory.
> Revere him, Israel's sons. *R.*

A reading from the letter of St Paul to the Philippians
Jesus assumed the condition of a slave.

His state was divine, yet Christ Jesus did not cling to his equality with God but emptied himself to assume the condition of a slave, and became as men are, and being as all men are, he was humbler yet, even to accepting death, death on a cross.

But God raised him high and gave him the name which is above all other names so that all beings in the heavens, on earth and in the underworld, should bend the knee at the name of Jesus and that every tongue should acclaim Jesus Christ as Lord, to the glory of God the Father.
This is the word of the Lord.

Praise to you, O Christ, king of eternal glory:
Christ was humbler yet,
even to accepting death, death on a cross.
But God raised him high
and gave him the name which is above all names.
Praise to you, O Christ, king of eternal glory.

The passion of our Lord Jesus Christ according to Matthew
(Shorter form)
The passion of Jesus reveals God's love for us.

Jesus was brought before Pontius Pilate, the governor, and the governor put to him this question, 'Are you the king of the Jews?' Jesus replied, 'It is you who say it.' But when he was accused by the chief priests and the elders he refused to answer at all. Pilate then said to him, 'Do you not hear how many charges they have brought against you?' But to the governor's complete amazement, he offered no reply to any of the charges.

At festival time it was the governor's practice to release a prisoner for the people, anyone they chose. Now there was at that time a notorious prisoner whose name was Barabbas. So when the crowds gathered, Pilate said to them, 'Which do you want me to release to you: Barabbas or Jesus, who is called

Christ?' For Pilate knew it was out of jealousy that they had handed him over.

Now as he was seated in the chair of judgement, his wife sent him a message, 'Have nothing to do with that man; I have been upset all day by a dream I had about him.'

The chief priests and the elders, however, had persuaded the crowd to demand the release of Barabbas and the execution of Jesus. So when the governor spoke and asked them, 'Which of the two do you want me to release for you?' they said, 'Barabbas.' 'But in that case,' Pilate said to them, 'what am I to do with Jesus who is called Christ?' They all said, 'Let him be crucified!' 'Why?' he asked, 'What harm has he done?' But they shouted all the louder, 'Let him be crucified!'

Then Pilate saw that he was making no impression, that in fact a riot was immanent. So he took some water, washed his hands in front of the crowd and said, 'I am innocent of this man's blood. It is your concern.' And the people to a man, shouted back, 'His blood be on us and on our children!' Then he released Barabbas for them. He ordered Jesus to be first scourged and then handed over to be crucified.

The governor's soldiers took Jesus with them into the Praetorium and collected the whole cohort round him. Then they stripped him and made him wear a scarlet cloak, and having twisted some thorns into a crown they put this on his head and placed a reed in his right hand. To make fun of him they knelt to him saying, 'Hail, king of the Jews!' And they spat on him and took the reed and struck him on the head with it. And when they had finished making fun of him, they took off the cloak and dressed him in his own clothes and led him away to crucify him.

On their way out, they came across a man from Cyrene, Simon by name, and enlisted him to carry his cross. When they had reached a place called Golgotha, that is, the place of the skull, they gave him wine to drink mixed with gall, which he tasted but refused to drink. When they had finished crucifying him they shared out his clothing by casting lots, and then sat down and stayed there keeping guard over him.

Above his head was placed the charge against him; it read: 'This is Jesus, the King of the Jews.' At the same time two robbers were crucified with him, one on the right and one on the left. The passers-by jeered at him; they shook their heads and said, 'So you would destroy the Temple and rebuild it in three days! Then save yourself! If you are God's son, come down from the cross!' The chief priests with the scribes and elders mocked him in the same way. 'He saved others,' they said, 'he cannot save himself. He is the king of Israel; let him come down from the cross now, and we will believe in him. He put his trust in God; now let God rescue him if he wants him. For he did say, "I am the son of God."' Even the robbers who were crucified with him taunted him in the same way.

From the sixth hour there was darkness over all the land until the ninth hour. And about the ninth hour, Jesus cried out in a loud voice, 'Eli, Eli, lama sabachthani?' that is, 'My God, my God, why have you deserted me?' When some of those who stood there heard this, they said, 'The man is calling on Elijah,' and one of them quickly ran to get a sponge which he dipped in vinegar and putting it on a reed, gave it him to drink. 'Wait!' said the rest of them 'and see if Elijah will come to save him.' But Jesus again crying out in a loud voice, yielded up his spirit. *(Pause)*

At that, the veil of the Temple was torn in two from top to bottom; the earth quaked; the rocks were split; the tombs opened and the bodies of many holy men rose from the dead, and these, after his resurrection, came out of the tombs, entered the Holy City and appeared to a number of people.

Meanwhile the centurion, together with the others guarding Jesus, had seen the earthquake and all that was taking place, and they were terrified and said, 'In truth this was a son of God.'
The usual response is not said.

MONDAY OF HOLY WEEK

Jesus dies and rises for us

A reading from the holy Gospel according to John
Six days before the Passover, Jesus went to Bethany, where Lazarus was, whom he had raised from the dead. They gave a dinner for him there; Martha waited on them and Lazarus was among those at table. Mary brought in a pound of very costly ointment, pure nard, and with it anointed the feet of Jesus, wiping them with her hair; the house was full of the scent of the ointment.

Jesus knows his hour has come
Mary anoints the feet of Jesus and he interprets this anointing as a preparation for his death and burial. He is already aware of how events will unfold. He already knows what lies before him. Yet he chooses to go forward because his Father has sent him to announce the saving plan of God's love to us.

Personal Exercise
At the beginning of this most holy of weeks, choose to set aside a bit more time than usual to meditate upon the mysteries of salvation revealed in the events of the last week of Jesus' earthly life.

Lenten Prayer
Let us prayer for the grace to mine the depths of God's love revealed to us through the suffering, passion, death and resurrection of Jesus.
We ask this through Christ our Lord. Amen.

The Son of Man is going to be handed over into the power of men; they will put him to death, and on the third day he will be raised to life again. *Matthew 17:21, 22*

Jesus dies and rises for us

A reading from the holy Gospel according to John
While at supper with his disciples, Jesus was troubled in spirit and declared, 'I tell you most solemnly, one of you will betray me.' The disciples looked at one another, wondering which he meant. The disciple Jesus loved was reclining next to Jesus; Simon Peter signed to him and said, 'Ask who it is he means', so leaning back on Jesus' breast he said, 'Who is it, Lord?' 'It is the one,' replied Jesus, 'to whom I give the piece of bread that I shall dip in the dish.' He dipped the piece of bread and gave it to Judas son of Simon Iscariot.

Jesus knows he is going to be betrayed
As events unfold Jesus reveals how much he is aware of the inner workings of his disciples. Although he knows betrayal is going to happen he is still deeply troubled in his spirit. Jesus knows Judas is merely the first to betray him. In a short time the others will follow suit.

Personal Exercise
Try to imagine the type and depth of love Jesus embodies when he knows he is going to be betrayed by one of his disciples yet chooses to see his mission through to the end.

Lenten Prayer
Let us pray that our spirit may be free from trouble by rooting ourselves totally in the love of God.
We ask this through Christ our Lord. Amen.

Let us love one another since love comes from God. *1 John 4:7*

WEDNESDAY OF HOLY WEEK

Jesus dies and rises for us

A reading from the holy Gospel according to Matthew
One of the Twelve, the man called Judas Iscariot, went to the chief priests and said, 'What are you prepared to give me if I hand him over to you?' They paid him thirty silver pieces, and from that moment he looked for an opportunity to betray him.

Words betray the heart
Judas' words to the chief priests lay bare his heartfelt intention of betraying Jesus. At this moment, as if to highlight the issue of integrity, Judas comes to represent a heart of darkness that is capable of betraying the heart of light – the Lord Jesus. Hence Judas keeps before us a truth that is both awesome and frightening: each one of us ever possesses the power to betray or to remain faithful to our Lord Jesus Christ.

Personal Exercise
Stay as loyal as you can to the person of Jesus by showing love to others in thought, word, and deed.

Lenten Prayer
Let us pray for the integrity to stay loyal to all that Christ is, and all he represents.
We ask this through Christ our Lord. Amen.

For where your treasure is, there will your heart be also.
Matthew 6:21

Jesus dies and rises for us

A reading from the holy Gospel according to John
It was before the festival of the Passover, and Jesus knew that the hour had come for him to pass from this world to the Father. He had always loved those who were his in the world, but now he showed how perfect his love was.

They were at supper, and the devil had already put it into the mind of Judas Iscariot son of Simon to betray him. Jesus knew that the Father had put everything into his hands, and that he had come from God and was returning to God, and he got up from table, removed his outer garment and, taking a towel, wrapped it round his waist; he then poured water into a basin and began to wash the disciples' feet and to wipe them with the towel he was wearing.

Jesus came to show us loving service
When Jesus washes the feet of his disciples he announces the message that he is by providing concrete example of the love of God. Love is to be practical, humble, and of service to one's fellow human beings who are made in the image of God.

Personal Exercise
Follow the example of Jesus by serving other people in love as often as you can.

Lenten Prayer
Let us pray for the courage to be humble enough to serve one another as the Lord Jesus has served us.
We ask this through Christ our Lord. Amen.

Serve one another in works of love. *Galatians 5:13*

Jesus dies and rises for us

A reading from the passion of our Lord Jesus Christ according to John
Near the cross of Jesus stood his mother and his mother's sister, Mary the wife of Clopas, and Mary of Magdala. Seeing his mother and the disciple he loved standing near her, Jesus said to his mother, 'Woman, this is your son.' Then to the disciple he said, 'This is your mother.' And from that moment the disciple made a place for her in his home.

After this, Jesus knew that everything had now been completed, and to fulfil the scripture perfectly he said: 'I am thirsty.' A jar full of vinegar stood there, so putting a sponge soaked in the vinegar on a hyssop stick they held it up to his mouth. After Jesus had taken the vinegar he said, 'It is accomplished'; and bowing his head he gave up his spirit.

Jesus surrenders his life out of love for us
Jesus – the Son of God, the Prince of Peace, the light of the world, the Alpha and the Omega – has humbled himself and given up his life so that we might share in the love of God.

Personal Exercise
Give praise to the Father for the gift of his Son.

Lenten Prayer
Let us pray in gratitude to realise how much the Son humbled himself to come among us and give his life so that we might become the children of God.
We ask this through Christ our Lord. Amen.

Jesus was humbler yet, even to accepting death, death on a cross. *Philippians 2:8*

Jesus dies and rises for us

A reading from the holy Gospel according to Matthew
After the sabbath, and towards dawn on the first day of the week, Mary of Magdala and the other Mary went to visit the sepulchre. And all at once there was a violent earthquake, for the angel of the Lord, descending from heaven, came and rolled away the stone and sat on it. His face was like lightning, his robe white as snow. The guards were so shaken, so frightened of him, that they were like dead men. But the angel spoke: and he said to the women, 'There is no need for you to be afraid. I know you are looking for Jesus, who was crucified. He is not here, for he has risen, as he said he would.'

Jesus fulfils his own prophecy
Jesus, the Word of God, possesses total integrity. The Good News for us is that he is risen from the dead as he said he would. Now he lives among us through the gift of his Holy Spirit through whom we share in the love of God.

Personal Exercise
Become more sensitive to the places in your life where the love of God comes upon you like the morning dawn.

Lenten Prayer
Let us pray for a greater sensitivity to the presence of the risen Lord in our lives and for the ability to respond to that presence. We ask this through Christ our Lord. Amen.

I am the resurrection and the life. *John 11:25*

GROUP MEETING

To review our spiritual journey through the Season of Lent

Gathering as the tiny Church.
Some moments of relaxation and becoming quiet.

Questions for sharing in dialogue
Our spiritual journey through Lent was undertaken so that we might grow in our understanding of what the death and resurrection of Jesus means for us. It also provided us with the opportunity to convert more to the ways of the Lord. In what ways have you been spiritually renewed during this Lenten season? How has Jesus and his Holy Spirit guided you ever deeper into the Father's love? How have you become a more loving person? How have you grown in your understanding of what the death and resurrection of Jesus means for you?
Relaxing music to be played as you reflect on your spiritual journey through Lent to allow you to discover meaning through, with, and in the risen Lord Jesus.

From dialogue to praise
Once relevant reflections and dialogue have been shared the person leading the session says: We have journeyed together through the time of Lent and grown in our understanding of what the dying and rising of Jesus means for us. We know Jesus is risen; we know he is with us always.

Liturgical Memory
We thank the living God for the gift of growing together in love through the Season of Lent. With grateful hearts we pray:
    Father, all-powerful and ever-living God,
    we do well always and everywhere to give you thanks
    through Jesus Christ our Lord.
    Each year you give us this joyful season
    when we prepare to celebrate the paschal mystery
    with mind and heart renewed.

You give us a spirit of loving reverence for you, our Father,
and of willing service to our neighbour.
As we recall the great events that gave us a new life in Christ,
you bring the image of your Son to perfection within us.
Now, with angels and archangels,
And the whole company of heaven,
We sing the unending hymn of your praise:
Holy, holy, holy…

Living Word
With deep gratitude we remember the risen Lord has walked with us on our journey through Lent and guided us to grow in the way of God's love. And so we hear his voice echo once more in our mind and heart: I am with you always.

(Name), Jesus speaks these words to you: I am with you always.

Quiet time/Intercessions

Closing Prayer
Let us pray with confidence in the words of the risen Lord: Our Father…

Blessing
Lord, make us more aware of your presence among us.
May we follow you in humility and truth.
We ask this in the name of Jesus the Lord. Amen.

The Lord grant us a quiet night and a perfect end. Amen.